SHARKS

Heinemann Library
Chicago, Illinois

Carol Baldwin

© 2003 Heinemann Library
a division of Reed Elsevier Inc.
Chicago, Illinois

Customer Service 888-454-2279

Visit our website at www.heinemannlibrary.com

Designed by Kimberly Saar, Heinemann Library
Illustrations and maps by John Fleck
Photo research by Bill Broyles
Originated by Amabassador Litho Ltd.
Printed in China by WKT

07 06 05 04
10 9 8 7 6 5 4 3 2

Library of Congress Cataloging-in-Publication Data
Baldwin, Carol, 1943-
  Sharks / Carol Baldwin.
    p. cm. -- (Sea creatures)
Summary: Discusses the life of sharks, describing where they live, what they eat, how they behave, and how humans study them.
Includes bibliographical references (p.   ).
  ISBN 1-40340-958-7 (HC), 1-4034-3566-9 (pbk.)
  1. Sharks--Juvenile literature. [1. Sharks.] I. Title. II. Series.
  QL638.9 .B345 2003
  597.3--dc21

                        2002010625

Acknowledgments
The author and publishers are grateful to the following for permission to reproduce copyright material:

Cover photograph by David B. Fleetham/Visuals Unlimited

Title page, p. 24 David B. Fleetham/Visuals Unlimited; p. 4 Bob Cranston/Seapics.com; p. 6 Mark Conlin/Seapics.com; p. 7 Ron & Valerie Taylor/Seapics.com; pp. 8, 18, 21, 22 Jeffrey Rotman Photography; pp. 9 Phillip Colla/Seapics.com; p. 10 James D. Watt/Visuals Unlimited; pp. 11L, 12 Richard Herrmann/Visuals Unlimited; pp. 11R, 13, 19, 23, 27 Doug Perrine/Seapics.com; p. 14 Nick Caloyianis/National Geographic Society; p. 15 Marty Snyderman/Seapics.com; p. 16 Amos Nachoum/Seapics.com; p. 17T Howard Hall/Seapics.com; p. 17B Glen Lowe/Seapics.com; p. 20 Jeffrey C. Carrier/Seapics.com; p. 25 Monterey Bay National Marine Sanctuary; p. 26 Richard T. Nowitz/Corbis; p. 28 Daniel Gotshall/Visuals Unlimited; p. 29 Bruce Rasner/Seapics.com

Special thanks to Dr. James Gelsleichter for his help in the preparation of this book.

Every effort has been made to contact copyright holders of any material reproduced in this book. Any omissions will be rectified in subsequent printings if notice is given to the publisher.

Some words are shown in bold, **like this.** You can find out what they mean by looking in the glossary.

Contents

Where Would You Find a Shark?

The boat drops its anchor near Darwin Island. You are 600 miles off the west coast of South America. You have come to the Galapagos Islands to see sharks. You put on your **SCUBA** gear and jump into the water. You swim out across a reef and start to move down the side of the reef's coral walls into deeper water.

Immediately, you notice a group of hammerhead sharks gliding through the water. Their wide, flat heads sweep from side to side. Soon, more hammerheads are swimming around you. Most of them are more than twice as long as you are tall.

You try to get closer to take a picture. But your bubbles seem to scare off the sharks. Finally, you swim back up to the surface.

The hammerhead shark's eyes and nostrils are at the tips of the flat "hammer."

What Kind of Creature is a Shark?

Sharks are fish, just as goldfish or guppies are. There are more than 25,000 kinds, or **species**, of fish in the world today.

Sharks are like other fish

Like all fish, sharks must live in water all the time. They also have a **backbone** to support their bodies. Sharks and other fish have fins for swimming and breathe through **gills.** Gills make it possible for fish to get oxygen from the water.

Sharks are different from bony fish

In some ways, sharks are different from other kinds of fish. Bony fishes, such as tunas and trout, have a skeleton make of bone, just like you do. But a shark's skeleton is made of **cartilage,** like the end of your nose. Cartilage usually isn't as hard as bone. However, in the shark's backbone, it is almost as hard as bone.

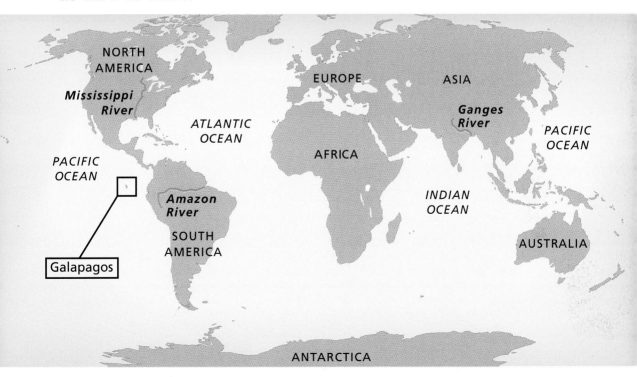

The small fish shown here have skeletons made of hard bone, but the white-tipped reef shark, like all sharks, does not.

Bony fish can swim forward and backward. But sharks can only swim forward. A bony fish has a swim bladder inside its body. This bladder is a bag filled with gas. It helps the fish float in the water. Sharks do not have swim bladders.

Bony fish also have large flaps that cover their **gill** slits. Sharks don't have gill covers. The skin of a bony fish is covered with slippery scales. A shark's skin is covered with small, toothlike scales that make its skin feel like sandpaper.

How Many Kinds of Sharks Are There?

About 400 different kinds, or **species,** of sharks are known. Sharks are divided into eight main groups. The first four groups of sharks include those you think of when you hear the word *shark.*

Bullhead sharks
Bullhead sharks have large, thick heads. They have turned up **snouts** and short mouth openings.

Mackerel sharks and carpet sharks
These two groups of large sharks include basking sharks and great white sharks. They have very long **snouts.** Their mouths open so wide that the opening reaches further back than the eyes. Carpet sharks include nurse sharks, whale sharks, and wobbegongs.

Ground sharks
The fourth group includes hammerhead sharks, blacktip sharks, and many of the species people usually see in **aquariums.** This is the biggest group. There are about 200 known species in it.

Whale sharks are the biggest fish in the ocean. They can grow up to 46 feet (14 meters) long. That's longer than a school bus.

Angel sharks

Angel sharks have flattened bodies like stingrays. This lets them hide in the sand on the ocean bottom.

Sawsharks

Sawsharks have long, flat snouts with slender, sharp teeth on the sides. They use their snouts to harm their **prey** before they eat it. Sawsharks prefer to live on the sand and mud floor of the ocean floor in shallow water.

Dogfish sharks

Dogfish include cookiecutter sharks, Greenland sharks, and spined pygmy sharks. Dogfish sharks live in oceans all over the world. Some of them live as deep as 20,000 feet (6,000 meters). That's almost four miles. It would take you about an hour to walk that far.

Frilled sharks and cow sharks

Frilled sharks and cow sharks include sixgill sharks, sevengill sharks, frilled sharks, and cow sharks. Scientists don't know too much about these two groups.

Shark relatives

Skates and rays are closely related to sharks. Like sharks, they have a skeleton made of **cartilage**. Their flattened bodies have large winglike fins joined to their heads.

The long, wide fins of the angel shark gave it its name.

What Are the Parts of a Shark's Body?

Sharks are **adapted** to life in the oceans. They have many body parts that help them live there.

Sense organs

As a shark swims, water flows into its nostrils. From there, water enters special **olfactory organs.** Sharks can smell very weak odors. A shark can smell one drop of blood in 25 gallons (95 liters) of seawater.

The pits on a shark's head can sense the heartbeat of a fish buried in the sand.

Small pits cover parts of the skin near a shark's nose and mouth. These pits can sense weak electrical signals given off by all animals. This helps a shark find food.

Most sharks see well, even at night, and some can see colors. Sharks' eyes have upper and lower eyelids. But they don't move, so sharks can't blink. Some sharks have a third eyelid. It can be closed to protect the shark's eye. A great white shark doesn't have a third eyelid. So it rolls its eyes back in its head to protect them while feeding.

A shark has a line of special cells under its skin along the sides of its body. This **lateral line** goes from its head to its tail. These cells help a shark sense movement and find food. The lateral line also helps a shark stay away from animals that might eat it.

Teeth, teeth, and more teeth

In most sharks, the mouth is below their **snout.** When a shark starts to bite, its snout bends up and out of the way. Its jaws move forward and stick out. When the shark bites, the jaws move back and under the snout. All this happens very fast.

Most sharks have five to fifteen rows of teeth in each jaw. When a tooth falls out, another tooth moves in to take its place. A missing tooth can be replaced in as little as 24 hours. Most sharks have teeth with very sharp points.

Skin

A shark's skin is covered by a layer of tiny toothlike scales. As a shark grows, it sheds these scales. They are replaced by slightly larger ones. Rubbing a shark's skin can scrape your hand.

This great white shark is preparing to bite. Great white sharks have the biggest teeth of any shark. They are nearly 3 inches (7.6 centimeters) high.

Many sharks' bodies are darker on top and lighter on the bottom. This is called **countershading.** Countershading is a kind of **camouflage** that makes an animal harder to see. If you look at them from below, their light bellies blend with the light above the water. If you look at them from above, their dark backs blend in with the seafloor.

Mako sharks are one kind of shark that has countershading.

Wobbegong sharks live in coral reefs near Australia. They use their camouflage to hide on the ocean bottom and wait for fish to swim by.

Some sharks that live on the bottom are also camouflaged. The wobbegong shark is hidden by its coloring and many flaps of skin at the sides of its body. The flaps help hide the outline of its body. It lies on the seafloor waiting for food to come near.

? Did you know?

People used to use shark skin for sandpaper. If you rub sandpaper on a bumpy surface, it will make it smooth.

Gill slits

Gill slits are long, narrow openings behind a shark's head. Most sharks have five pairs of gill slits, but some have six or seven pairs. As a shark breathes, water goes into its mouth and passes over its gills. Oxygen in the water goes into the shark's blood that is in the gills. Carbon dioxide from the shark's blood passes out of the gills and into the water. The water then goes out through the gill slits.

This blue shark has one dorsal fin. The pectoral fins are much larger than the pelvic fins.

Fins

A shark has two pairs of fins on its sides. The **pectoral fins** are just behind or below its gill slits. **Pelvic fins** are near the rear of its body. A shark also has one or two **dorsal fins** on its back and a tail fin. Some sharks also have an **anal fin** underneath near the tail.

Where Do Sharks Live?

Sharks live in oceans all over the world. A few even live in rivers. But they live in different **habitats** within Earth's waters.

Ocean sharks

Many kinds of sharks can be found in the Atlantic, Pacific, and Indian Oceans. These include hammerheads, whale sharks, great white sharks, tiger sharks, thresher sharks, and mako sharks. Galapagos sharks stay near islands in these oceans. Greenland sharks live only in the Arctic and northern Atlantic Oceans. And salmon sharks seem to be the only sharks found in the ocean around Antarctica. Any others haven't been discovered, yet.

Bull sharks in Lake Nicaragua in Central America travel between the lake and the ocean.

River sharks

River sharks live in rivers all the time. One kind lives in the Ganges River in India. Another kind was found in a river in Malaysia. River sharks are very rare, and little is known about them. In fact, some kinds were thought to be **extinct.** But in the late 1990s, researchers once again found them.

Lemon sharks and tiger sharks spend most of their time in the ocean. However, they sometimes travel a short distance into rivers from the ocean. Bull sharks are often found in rivers and some lakes. They have been found far up the Mississippi River and the Amazon River in South America.

Sharks live in warm and cold habitats

Tiger sharks, nurse sharks, and hammerheads live in warm water. Basking sharks, mako sharks, and thresher sharks live in **temperate** water that's not too warm or too cold. Goblin sharks live in cold, deep water, far from land. And Greenland sharks swim in the cold, dark water under the Arctic ice.

Highs and lows—surface, bottom, and deep water sharks

Basking sharks and whale sharks spend most of their time near the ocean's surface because that's where their food is. They eat **zooplankton.** Whale sharks also spend a lot of time at the surface, and they swim so slowly that they have even been hit by ships.

? **Did you know?**

Sharks are one of Earth's oldest living groups of animals. The first sharks appeared about 400 million years ago, even before the dinosaurs.

The slow-moving Greenland shark lives in water that's only 28 °F (−2 °C).

*Nurse sharks have small mouths. They can press their thick lips over a hole and suck out their **prey**.*

Nurse sharks prefer to stay near the bottom of shallow water. They move very little during the day and eat at night. Spined pygmy sharks spend their days in water as deep as 6,550 feet (2,000 meters). At night, they swim up to find food.

On the move—migration

Sharks that **migrate** do so for three main reasons. They may move to special areas where they lay their eggs or produce their young. They might need to follow their food source, which has also migrated. Or they might migrate if the water becomes too warm or too cold. Some sharks migrate long distances. Bull sharks in South America migrate thousands of miles each year from the Amazon River to the Atlantic Ocean. Blue sharks and mako sharks migrate across entire oceans.

What Do Sharks Eat?

Different kinds of sharks eat different things. Most are carnivores and eat meat. Some sharks eat **zooplankton.** Others will eat just about anything!

Some sharks hunt food

Some sharks are fast-moving **predators.** They catch and eat **prey** such as fish, squid, seals, and even other sharks. Fast-moving sharks include great whites, makos, hammerheads, and tiger sharks. Tiger sharks are well known for eating strange things. Scientists have found bottles, coats, and bags of potatoes in their stomachs.

Other sharks are slow-moving predators. Sharks like angel sharks and wobbegongs crush and eat animals that live on the sea floor. They eat animals like small fish, clams, and crabs. Nurse sharks have special whiskerlike organs on their lower jaws. These help them find food like sea snails that are buried in the sand.

Thresher sharks may use their long tails to slap and stun their prey. They have small, but very sharp teeth.

16

This basking shark can strain food from over 25 gallons (95 liters) of water each minute.

Some sharks strain their food

Some sharks feed only on tiny bits of zooplankton and fish eggs that float in the ocean. Whale sharks and basking sharks swim through the water with their mouths open. When they close their mouths, special parts of their gills strain the food from the water they take in. The water goes out their gill slits and they swallow the food. These sharks have to eat huge amounts of these tiny food items.

What are Cookie Cutter Sharks?

Cookie cutter sharks are about two feet long. They attack large fish and whales. Cookie cutters attach their mouths to prey like suction cups. Then they use sawlike teeth that move back and forth to take a round bite of flesh. They punch out a hole from their prey like a cookie cutter pressed into a sheet of dough. The wound is about the size of an ice-cream scoop.

What Do We Know About Shark Behavior?

Many details of sharks' lives remain a mystery. Most species are hard to study. They travel quickly over long distances. Many live in deep water. Still, scientists have learned some things about sharks.

Most sharks live alone

Many sharks usually live and hunt by themselves. They only join up with other sharks for **mating.** But there are **species,** such as hammerheads, that form large groups, or schools. Scientists aren't sure why they behave this way.

White-tipped reef sharks travel and hunt in large groups.

Sometimes sevengill sharks work together to hunt fur seals. Sevengill sharks are between four and five feet (one to one and a half meters) long. A large fur seal is too big for one shark to kill. So a group of sharks forms a wide ring around a single seal. They slowly move in. When they get close, one shark will suddenly attack. The rest follow, and they all get a meal.

Tiger sharks are one type of shark that is known to attack people.

Sharks don't normally attack people

Before they eat something, many sharks give it a test bite. Sometimes a shark may mistake a person's movements for those of fish or seals, and people are bitten by mistake. The shark makes one grab, lets go, and leaves.

But some sharks are dangerous to people. These sharks may circle and bump a person before biting. Or, in deeper water they may swim up from below. These kinds of attacks can cause serious injury or death. Here are some ways that you can avoid a shark attack:

• Never swim alone, especially at night, dawn, or dusk.
• Don't swim too far from shore.
• Don't go into the water if you're bleeding.
• Don't wear shiny jewelry or bright clothing.
• Don't splash a lot.
• If you see a shark, get out of the water.

What Is Shark Family Life Like?

Sharks don't live in family groups. Many sharks come together only for **mating.**

Sharks mate

People who study sharks don't often get a chance to see their mating behavior. Scientists got lucky during one five-week period off the coast of the Florida Keys. During that time, they watched about twenty nurse sharks in the shallow water of the coral reefs.

First a male nurse shark swims up to a female. He grabs a female's **pectoral fin** with his mouth. Then he tows her to deeper water. He rolls the female over and puts his tail underneath her. A male shark has two **claspers,** one on each **pelvic fin.** He inserts one clasper into the female's body to fertilize her eggs. After mating, a female shark becomes pregnant. Most large sharks are **pregnant** for about twelve months.

Females often have wounds on their pectoral fins and the sides of their bodies after mating.

A newborn nurse shark looks like a tiny adult. This baby was born with its yolk sac still attached.

Some sharks lay eggs

Many species of sharks lay eggs. Sharks that lay eggs are called **oviparous.** Catsharks are oviparous. The eggs are usually attached to rocks in the water. Catshark eggs are one to two inches (two to five centimeters) long. The eggs have to survive for weeks or months until they hatch. Inside each egg, the **embryo** is connected to a yolk sac, which provides food. When the eggs hatch, the young sharks, called pups, must survive on their own.

Most sharks give birth

Sharks such as nurse sharks and great white sharks are **ovoviviparous.** They have eggs that grow inside the mother's body. Yolk sacs give the embryos food. The eggs hatch inside the mother. In the great white shark, the young eat any unfertilized eggs in the mother's body. When the mother gives birth, the pups swim away and must take care of themselves.

Bull sharks and hammerheads are **viviparous.** They have **embryos** that grow inside the mother's body, but not in egg cases. **Nutrients** from the mother's blood pass through the **placenta** to the embyros. When the embryos are grown, the mother gives birth. Sand tiger shark young may even eat their littermates. Sand tiger sharks usually give birth to only two pups at a time. Blue sharks might have more than a hundred.

Baby sharks grow up

Many females give birth close to shore. Galapagos shark pups stay in shallow water when they are very young. This helps them avoid being eaten by the adult sharks. Young bull sharks stay in bays near the mouths of rivers. Those that are lucky will live long enough to mate.

Young sharks, like these baby hammerhead sharks, live in a dangerous world.

Do Whale Sharks Lay Eggs?

In 1953, a 14.5-inch (37-centimeter) whale shark embryo was taken from an egg case found floating in the Gulf of Mexico. That suggested that whale sharks were **oviparous.** However, in 1996 a fisherman caught a female who had 300 embryos in her body. The pups were each about two feet long. So this means that whale sharks are **ovoviviparous.**

Are Sharks Endangered?

Many kinds of sharks are in danger from people. They are being killed faster than they can **reproduce.**

This hammerhead is one of more than 200 million sharks killed each year by commercial fishing, sport fishing, finning, and accidents.

Sharks are killed for food

In many parts of the world, sharks are caught for their meat. Other sharks are killed just for their fins. Sharks are caught and pulled onto a boat. Their fins are cut off. This is called **finning.** The wounded sharks are thrown back into the water. Without fins, they can't swim. They sink to the bottom and die. The fins are sold to make soup that costs about $100 a bowl.

Sharks are killed by accident

Many fishing boats use huge nets that catch everything in their paths. Sharks caught in the nets are injured. Other sharks are caught by long fishing lines that have many hooks. People on fishing boats throw wounded sharks back into the water. Many of them die.

Sharks are killed for sport

In many places, charter boats take people into the ocean to fish for sharks. Blue, mako, and thresher sharks are caught near Massachusetts. Off Texas, people catch bull, tiger, and hammerhead sharks. People may have the sharks mounted as trophies. Or they just keep the shark's jaws. Some people eat the meat from the sharks they catch, but most do not. One private fishing boat can catch as many as 40 sharks in a day.

Sharks are killed for body parts

Sharks have been killed for the oil that is in their livers. Shark oil is sometimes used in make-up, such as lipstick. Sharks have also been killed for their skin. The skin is tanned into leather to make shoes and clothing. Shark jaws and teeth are sold for decorations or jewelry. And shark **cartilage** is used in medicines for people and pets.

Shark jaws are lined up for sale in a souvenir shop.

Setting aside special places to protect sharks will also protect other sea life.

Saving sharks

Sharks play an important role in the oceans. They help keep the numbers of other fish **species** in balance. People must take action to help save sharks before they disappear. Some things that need to be done include:

• Do not allow people to kill sharks. For example, great white sharks are now protected in some parts of the world.

• Protect coastal areas where young sharks and other young fish live and grow.

• Make shark **finning** against the law. Australia and the United States now have laws that do this.

• Change fishing methods to reduce the number of sharks that are accidentally killed.

• Encourage people not to buy things made from sharks.

How Do We Learn About Sharks?

Some things about sharks, such as how their bodies are put together, can be learned from studying dead sharks that are caught on purpose or by accident. But scientists need to study living sharks to understand their behavior.

*In North America, more than 100 million people visit public **aquariums** each year.*

The "Shark Lady"

Dr. Eugenie Clark has studied sharks for many years. She was born in New York and got interested in sharks when her mother took her to an aquarium. She studies sharks in aquariums and in the wild. She helped start the Mote Marine Laboratory, a leading center for shark research. We have learned a lot about sharks because of her research.

Scientists expect satellite tags will stay on a shark for one to two years.

Studying sharks in aquariums

Sharks can be observed in aquariums. But **captive** sharks do not behave the same way as sharks in the wild. They don't have to hunt for food or find a mate. And they don't have to avoid other **predators.** The best way to study sharks is in the wild.

Studying sharks in Australia

In Australia, scientists are tracking great white sharks as they swim. Special tags on the sharks' bodies radio their positions to a satellite. The satellite sends the information to a computer on the ground. Some of the things scientists hope to learn include where sharks go in different seasons; what places sharks use for feeding, breeding, and as nurseries; and how often sharks visit and how long they stay in different places.

Studying sharks around the world

Other studies are done by the Mote Marine Laboratory's Center for Shark Research (CSR) in Florida. People at CSR study sharks in many parts of the world. They study nursery areas in the Gulf of Mexico and Gulf of California. They also tag sharks to study **migration** and how fast sharks grow.

☑ Most sharks get water to pass over their gills by swimming forward. That means they stay in motion most of the time. But some sharks have a set of muscles that suck in water and push it past their gills. These sharks don't have to always swim in order to breathe.

A shark's egg case is called a mermaid's purse. It even has a "string" at the top to hold the "purse."

☑ Some sharks are like the ocean's garbage disposal. Opened shark's stomachs have held soft drink bottles, lead sinkers, old clothes, magazines, boat anchors, and tin cans.

☑ Tiger sharks can throw up things they didn't want to swallow by turning their stomachs inside out through their mouths.

☑ Some people think that sharks never get cancer. This is not true. They just don't get it very often. Cancer cells need a blood supply, and **cartilage** produces substances that slow the growth of blood vessels. Since shark skeletons are all cartilage, they make good study subjects for scientists who study cancer.

☑ Pills made from shark cartilage will not prevent cancer in people.

☑ The special substances in shark cartilage cannot be digested by humans.

☑ Mako sharks are the fastest swimmers of all sharks. They can travel faster than 30 miles (48 kilometers) per hour.

☑ Sharks have huge livers that are full of oil. A shark's liver can make up more than one-tenth of its body weight. The oil in a shark's liver helps it float in the water.

☑ In December 2000, the United States government passed a law that bans shark **finning** in all United States waters. Shark finning was also banned the same year in Australia.

☑ Although sharks rarely kill people, people kill about 20 to 30 million sharks each year.

☑ Scientists on the California coast tracked a great white shark as it swam to Hawaii. It swam 2,400 miles (3,900 kilometers) in only 40 days. That's 60 miles (100 kilometers) every day.

The first megamouth shark wasn't discovered until 1976. This 13- to 17-foot shark strains tiny zooplankton from the water. It also eats deep-sea shrimp.

Glossary

adapted changed to live under certain conditions

anal fin small fin on the back, bottom part of a shark

camouflage way an animal hides

captive an animal taken away from its natural habitat and held in another place

cartilage tough, flexible material that forms the skeleton of sharks

clasper rodlike part on male shark's pelvic fin used in mating

countershading an animal's body is darker on the top and lighter on the bottom

dorsal fin fin on the top of a shark's body

embryo animal during the time it grows from a fertilized egg until it can live on its own

extinct no longer existing on Earth

finning cutting the fins off live sharks

gill thin feathery organs on the sides of a fish's head through which it breathes

gill slit slit-like openings behind a shark's head

habitat place where an animal or plant lives

lateral line row of organs on the sides of fish that sense movement in the water

mating a male and female animal come together to reproduce and make babies

migrate move from place to place with the seasons

nutrient material that is needed for growth of a plant or animal

olfactory organs body parts that allow an animal to smell

oviparous produces eggs that hatch outside the mother's body

ovoviviparous produces eggs that hatch inside the mother's body

pectoral fins paired fins that are located just behind or below a fish's gill slits

pelvic fins paired fins that are located on a fish's sides near the rear of its body

placenta spongy organ by which an embryo get nutrients from the mother's bloodstream

predator animal that hunts and eats other animals

pregnant going to have a baby

prey animal that is hunted and eaten by other animals

reproduce produce offspring

SCUBA Self Contained Underwater Breathing Apparatus. This is the air tank, hose, and mouthpiece that allows divers to breathe underwater.

snout nose

species group of organisms that have the same characteristics

temperate not very hot and not very cold

vertebral column spine or backbone

viviparous produces living young, rather than eggs

zooplankton tiny animals that float near the surface of the water

More Books to Read

Butts, Ellen and Joyce Schwartz. *Eugenie Clark: Adventures of a Shark Scientist*. The Shoestring Press, Inc./Linnet Books, 2000.

Fitzgerald, Patrick J. *Shark Attacks*. Danbury, Conn.: Children's Press, 2000.

Levine, Marie. *Great White Sharks*. Austin, Tex.: Raintree Steck-Vaughn, 1997.

Lopez, Gary. *Sharks: Sea Life*. Chanhassen, Minn.: Child's World, 2001.

Strong, Mike. *Shark: The Truth Behind the Terror*. Mankato, Minn.: Capstone Press, 2002.

Index